Don't Dig So Deep, Nicholas!

TROON HARRISON · GARY CLEMENT

Owl Books

Owl Books are published by Greey de Pencier Books Inc.,
179 John Street, Suite 500, Toronto, Ontario M5T 3G5

OWL and the Owl colophon are trademarks of Owl Communications.
Greey de Pencier Books Inc. is a licensed user of trademarks of Owl Communications.

Distributed in the United States by Firefly Books (U.S.) Inc.,
230 Fifth Avenue, Suite 1607, New York, NY 10001.

This book was published with the generous support of the Canada Council,
the Ontario Arts Council and the Ontario Publishing Centre.

DEDICATION
"For my parents, with love" — T. H.
"To Sal, Haras and Mr. B." — G. C.

Cataloguing in Publication Data

Harrison, Troon
Don't dig so deep, Nicholas

ISBN 1-895688-51-5 (bound) ISBN 1-895688-60-4 (pbk)

I. Clement, Gary. II. Title.

PS8565.A658D6 1997   jC813'.54   C95-932576-X
PZ7.H37Do 1997

Design & Art Direction: Julia Naimska

Printed in Hong Kong

A   B   C   D   E   F

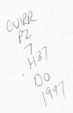

One day Nicholas took a blue shovel
to the beach and began to dig a hole. He
dug
and
he
dug.

A man in a deck chair looked over the top of his
newspaper. "If you keep digging like that," he said,
"You'll go right through to Australia."

Nicholas didn't answer. He was just too busy digging.
The pile of sand beside his hole grew larger and larger.

SUDDENLY

out of the hole leaped a huge red kangaroo with feet like rocking-chair rockers.

It soared over the man with the newspaper and the man's sleeping wife in one bound. Behind it came four more kangaroos, with joeys grinning in their pockets.

The kangaroos jumped over the picnic tables and the volleyball net. One gave the volleyball such a kick that it flew over the tree tops and out of sight.

Nicholas kept on digging.

SUDDENLY

up out of the hole ran a cinnamon-colored dingo dog with golden eyes and a tongue like pink ham. Four more dingos followed, all hot, hungry and running hard.

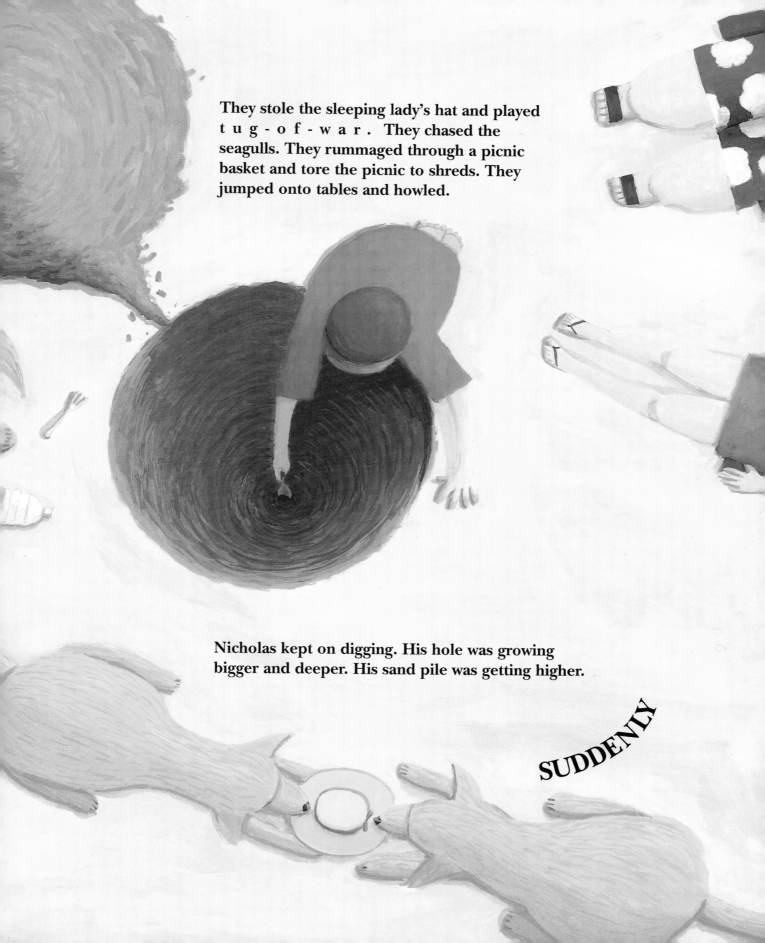

They stole the sleeping lady's hat and played
t u g - o f - w a r . They chased the
seagulls. They rummaged through a picnic
basket and tore the picnic to shreds. They
jumped onto tables and howled.

Nicholas kept on digging. His hole was growing
bigger and deeper. His sand pile was getting higher.

SUDDENLY

up out of the hole
lumbered a camel with a coat like an old shag rug.
Four more camels followed, and they were all
quite without any manners.

They walked on towels.
They spat at the people who
were looking for the lost volleyball.
One of them leaned over the sleeping lady and said

B–U–R–P!

in her ear.

Then they all lay down. They lay on a radio and muffled it. They lay on a sandcastle and squashed it. They lay on a bag of ham sandwiches and turned them into MUSH! Then they chewed their cud and stared.

Nicholas kept on digging.
The sand was cold and damp on the sides of his hole.

When a flock of kookaburras went winging past him, Nicholas barely looked up.

Next came a flock of white cockatoos with black beaks and eyes like currants.

The birds settled all over. The cockatoos chattered and the kookaburras laughed. Soon, people had to **shout** just to make themselves heard above the noise from the birds.

Nicholas went on digging.
It was quiet and shady in his deep sandy hole.

Five furry koalas
clambered out
carrying babies
on their backs.

They began to hunt for things to climb. The beach umbrella toppled onto the sleeping lady, who woke up with a shriek. While she struggled to get out, the koalas padded silently away.

Soon they began to **climb** on the volleyball net.

Four woolly wombats arrived next.
They grunted softly to Nicholas in the depths of the hole.

They were round and furry and expert diggers.
When they set to work with their long front claws, the sand began to fly.

Nicholas and the wombats dug together **magnificently**.

SUDDENLY, out through the flying sand appeared a procession of duckbilled platypuses.

They smiled at Nicholas with their bills, and set off across
the beach in search of water. On the way they collected
a striped ball, and a rubber ring, and a purple spotted
crocodile to play with in the waves. When they discovered
a small inflatable boat on the wet sand, they pushed it into
the water, too.

It made
an excellent
diving platform.

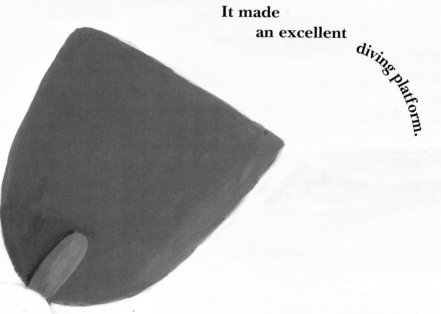

The platypuses swam happily.

On the shore, the dingos howled and the kangaroos bounced around like rubber balls. The camels belched and the kookaburras laughed. People searched under towels and behind bushes for their missing beach toys.

Nicholas kept on digging.
It was easier now that the wombats were helping him.

It was almost sunset when six silent wallabies appeared and passed Nicholas with shy eyes. Their fingers were clever and their curiosities were large. They picked through beach bags and pockets and purses; they played with keys and money and sunscreen. One of them found an apple to eat.

There was pandemonium everywhere.

Then, just at the very moment
that the sun touched the horizon,
silence fell over the beach.

The wombats stopped digging.
Nicholas popped his head out of his hole in the sand.
He watched as the huge red kangaroos came bounding back.

One by one they jumped over his head and disappeared down the hole.

Then the
koalas came,
carrying their babies.

The sleek,
wet platypuses
paddled out
of the waves.

The dingos
ran up over
Nicholas's sand pile
with their tongues
hanging out.

In the last orange light of the sun, all the animals returned to the hole.

The camels disappeared into it behind the dingos. The wallabies followed, dropping apple cores and wallets. The birds flew in, shrieking and calling. Soon only the wombats were left.

Nicholas climbed up
onto his great sand pile
and began to fill
the hole back in.

The wombats helped him.
They dug and grunted inside the hole. When the
hole was almost filled, it was time for the wombats to go home, too.
Nicholas waved good-bye with his blue shovel as they
hurried away down the tunnel.

On the whole beach,
there was nothing left of the animals
except footprints and a white cockatoo feather.

The man in the deck chair folded up his newspaper.
"See," he said to Nicholas, "I *told* you about digging through to Australia."

Nicholas didn't answer. He was too busy shovelling sand back into the hole.
When he was finished, he stamped on the sand to pack it down. Then he
walked away down the beach in the footsteps of dingos and wallabies,
whistling to himself as he went.

Nicholas' Australian Animals

Kangaroos are marsupials, which means that they
carry their young in a pouch. A baby kangaroo, about the size
of a peanut at birth, crawls into its mother's pouch and
doesn't come out for about four months.

Dingos, or wild dogs, are the only furry
Australian animals that aren't marsupials. They
probably descend from dogs brought to Australia
thousands of years ago by their aboriginal owners.

Koalas eat so many eucalyptus leaves that
they smell like strong cough drops. A koala lives
its whole life in eucalyptus trees, sleeping on
the lower branches.

Camels were brought to Australia to carry heavy loads
through the desert: they can go for days without water,
have wide feet to keep from sinking in the sand, and
can shut their nostrils to keep sand out of their noses.

Wombats carry their young in pouches
like kangaroos do. But a wombat's pouch opens
backwards towards its tail, so that dirt and
rocks won't get inside when it burrows.

Kookaburras kill snakes by dropping them
from the air, and then they eat them. The call of a
kookaburra sounds like a loud laugh.

A playtpus eats shrimp, worms and crayfish.
It stores them in its cheek pouches and, since it has
no teeth, chews them with its hard gums.

Cockatoos live a long time. There are stories
of cockatoos living more than 100 years, and they
usually live about as long as people do.

Wallabies are small kangaroos. If a kangaroo's
feet are shorter than 25 cm (10 inches) — about the
length of a new pencil — it is called a wallaby.